Backpacking

Travel The World!
Everything You Need to Know
about Backpacking from Beginner
to Expert

Larry Fisher

Larry Fisher

Legal Notice:

This e-book is copyright protected. This is only for personal use. You cannot amend, distribute, sell, use, quote or paraphrase any part or the content within this e-book without the consent of the author or copyright owner. Legal action will be pursued if this is breached.

Disclaimer Notice:

Please note the information contained within this document is for educational and entertainment purposes only. Every attempt has been made to provide accurate, up to date and reliable complete information. No warranties of any kind are expressed or implied. Readers acknowledge that the author is not engaging in the rendering of legal, financial, medical or professional advice.

By reading this document, the reader agrees that under no circumstances are we responsible for any losses, direct or indirect, which are incurred as a result of the use of information contained within this document, including, but not limited to, —errors, omissions, or inaccuracies.

Table of Contents

Larry Fisher

Introduction

Tired of the usual adventure? You may be used to certain accommodations of travel life that delve little beyond the standard expectations of hotels, room service, camping out, getting lost, getting back home...etc. etc. But what if you can have all of these and more for one grand adventure in a lifetime? The world has so much to offer and in reality, we do not all have the time in the world to explore it.

Yes! Feed into those instincts for a newfound sense of freedom and go on a backpacking trip to unleash your inner soul. Explore what your eyes have not yet seen, what your hands have not yet touched, your mouth not yet tasted, and your heart not yet appreciated. Take it one town after another, one city after another, and one country after another. Garner a sense of worldliness and well-roundedness that goes beyond clicks on the Internet and living vicariously through other people's stories. Reward yourself and enrich your life with a first-hand experience unlike any other that you will remember and revel in for years to come.

Well, when you make it happen for yourself, your life will never be the same. This is simply because once you have started backpacking, you will start to knit together an elaborate tapestry of all your experiences in one country after another, one city after another and so on. The more that you go backpacking, the deeper your understanding grows as to how the world works for others. Backpacking is invariably life enriching and life changing. The lessons you are bound to learn can never be taught by the greatest professors, the best books, even by your own loved ones because truly the best way to get to know and understand anything is by being open and courageous enough to experience it for yourself.

Now, what could be holding you back? It is possible that the idea can be just truly overwhelming in the beginning. Within the initial attempt, you may find yourself preparing too much or too little due to the absence of real experience. Most people would definitely know better the second time around by learning from mistakes, cultivating better preparation, and picking up little tricks and tips along the way. But if you are after a hassle-free backpacking experience, whether for your first or *nth* time, then this book can offer you the essentials that will put a smiley face on your backpacking journal and a refreshing zest for travel in your spirit.

Let this book usher you toward the fundamentals of packing up, buying, and taking the right gear to make your trip a dash more enjoyable, convenient, and a worthwhile memory. By reading on you will pick up points about international travel that will open up the world to you that you are exploring more than any stay at a hotel or cookie cutter tour can offer.

You will know what you need with this, information-packed, no nonsense, friendly book that will make you say WOW before, during, and after the backpacking trip. If you are all set to get started for your next backpacking adventure, read on, as you are about to embark on the backpacking crash course you certainly deserve.

As Saint Augustine once said, "The world is a book, and those who do not travel, read only a page." So get out there and see what the world has to offer.

Chapter 1

Know The Difference Between A Backpacker And A Glampacker

Funny how you may meet someone who would ask if you were a backpacker or a glampacker. For many who may respond with, 'Glam—what??' this reaction is entirely expected. So who exactly are these glampackers? And why does it even matter to know the difference between the two?

Well, if travelling light, spending wisely, and taking the right gear is your ultimate criteria for a worry-free backpacking adventure, then you should gauge yourself as to which one you are. Knowing the range of your comfort level while travelling is going to determine the bulk of your experience.

That is why it is best to get a glimpse beforehand of what you will be getting into in order to assure your most pleasurable experience without enduring entanglements, upsets or disappointments.

It is granted that nothing is an adventure without offering you a few surprises or the occasional curveball along the way. After all, being pushed a little beyond our comfort zone is what helps to grow our awareness and experiences, and makes things more memorable anyways. Being prepared with the right mentality and the right gear beforehand though will allow you to take those surprises in grace and perhaps amusement without them turning into a disaster that compromises the quality of your trip altogether. The world of backpacking has evolved so much over the past 10 years that certain practices have deviated a bit. So here are the basic differences between a glampacker and a backpacker.

The Glampacker

Glampackers tend to travel in style and they often go with a much bigger budget. These are the travelers who would not mind taking their Chanel summer dress when hitting a tropical country, or probably their loveliest pair of sandals to go walking with. They often travel with an extra carry-on bag for their cosmetics, shoes, accessories and what-not. In short, they really put the 'glamour' in backpacking travel.

Glampackers tend to over prepare, taking items along with them that they are attached to, thinking they will use them on their trip when really it just becomes an excess amount of stuff. This includes several outfits for different occasions, gadgets or electronics that are fun but become 'just in case-ers' in which that particular case never arises on the trip, or a handful of books that do not get read because the activities of the trip do not allow time for them. In many ways, these excessive objects really just serve as a sense of comfort and home that the traveler is leaving behind. They take these items with them as a way of taking a part of their home with them because the underlying concept of traveling to an unfamiliar place is somewhat discomforting. This tendency makes sense and is actually quite normal.

Glampackers often travel for a gap year and a career break. They do not mind staying at a hotel or renting out a posh apartment during this 'travel period'. When they plan to return, they need to hit up a souvenir shop for another batch of items to bring home, and sometimes another bag to bring it all in. Their travel period does not necessarily have to be for an entire year though; it can be for a week, a couple of weeks or a month. The point is that the lifestyle they are used to and have cut out for themselves lays heavily into their bank account. Also, it often shelters them from experiencing the vast array of opportunities and colorful milieu that stepping out of a secluded resort estate and off the high streets provides.

A glampacker will often go home bearing a lovely tan on the skin and a huge bag of goodies. She or he may be well-rested and ready to get back to the usual work and life routine. This person will often feel that they have had a wonderful vacation but it may not be considered a life-altering experience. Many times the activities of a glampacker will have just touched the surface of what immersing oneself in a different culture truly offers.

The Backpacker

Backpackers put comfort first when it comes to the choice of items to wear. They mostly go with the lightest cargo shorts, some kind of brimmed hat, or a cropped shirt. Walking shoes or sandals are a top choice also. Sunglasses and a head bandana are essentials for them, too. This is not to say that an experienced backpacker will often come off looking like some kind of mountaineer. The illustration to truly embrace is that they dress casually but for durability and practicality. Everything that a backpacker wears has a certain purpose to compliment the journey, although they are not without style. They can put everything they need for an entire month in a single day bag.

A smart backpacker will also dress somewhat accordingly to the couture of the native region that they are travelling in so as not to stick out entirely like a sore thumb. Sure, it is true that a backpacker's bodily physical appearance will give them away somewhat in comparison to the natives of the country they are exploring, depending on which country he or she chooses to go to. Not to mention that if he or she is carrying the backpack around with them it can easily identify them as a traveler. The difference is that by acclimating to some regard in the typical dress style of the country one is travelling, a backpacker is less likely to draw attention to themselves as a lost or bewildered tourist, which is the kind of target that pickpockets prey on. No need to fear though, we have got you covered and this type of danger to look out for is not as common as you may think. Later on in the book we will discuss preventative measures to assure that you do not become such a target. This is just one of them.

Backpackers do not isolate themselves in hotels or in private villas. They mostly rent out a room in a local's home, hostels, and/or the local community bed and breakfast. As they are keener on experiencing the ways of life in the local towns or cities they are visiting, you can expect them to stay in regular homes or smaller hotels. Thus, they get to stay longer and spend less. This also puts them right in the thick of the lifestyle of the country's inhabitants and culture. It is called 'cultural immersion,' and it is truly the only way to really get the most out of a travelling experience because a backpacker will then begin to see a hint of the way that people in that particular region view the world and why. This view gives a whole new depth to the appearance and purpose of that culture and it is what will enhance the backpacker's life; to see the world and purpose of doing things from different perspectives that adds to their understanding.

When a backpacker heads home, he or she brings a whole new perspective of life back with them, along with a greater appreciation for the differences and variety among the world. He or she can go back to his or her usual routine, although certain facets may have been changed forever.

A small but simple and practical example is that in the United States and certain other prominent countries, people are used to putting dirty dishes in the dishwasher or wash them by hand, but leave the faucet running the whole time which is ultimately a waste of water. People in these cultures are so accustomed to having an abundance of resources that they do not think or even need to think about what the actions of their lifestyles imply in a greater scheme.

And then say that a person native to one of these cultures goes backpacking over in a South American country or to Spain where they are prone to droughts and water shortages. A backpacker may stay at an accommodation in a local resident's home and witness them put soap and water in a shallow bowl or on each dish and get them wet with a small amount of water. They will keep the faucet off and wash each dish with this soap and water until they are clean, and only then will they turn the faucet back on to rinse each dish. They have developed this technique as a necessary means of living due to their living conditions, but it also serves as a way to cut down on the water bill and conserve on the consumption of water. Witnessing this could create a great impact on the backpacker, which may provoke them to adopt this method when they go back home.

Another fun example that a backpacker may experience in certain parts of Central and Eastern Europe is seeing that many cultures of this region celebrate the Christmas holiday over the course of three days instead of just one. The first day is reserved for the kids of the family to spend with their friends, the second day is spent with immediate family members and the third is spent together with extended family members. In this way the people who celebrate the Christmas holiday get to make the most out of it with all the loved ones that are important to them and remain immersed in the spirit that it brings.

So ultimately then the question is – which type of a traveler are you? If you chose the latter then keep on reading as this book can definitely help you embrace a whole new set of habits in backpacking with added efficiency and convenience.

Larry Fisher

Chapter 2

Keys To Travelling Light; Travelling Might

The sun is out already and you cannot contain the excitement of going on a backpacking trip. OK, do not pull out your snorkels and swimming fins just yet, or your huge bottle of sunscreen and your rubber shoes for an early jog on the beach. WOW! In a single minute you have managed to pull out the bulkiest items already. Unfortunately, there really may not be any room in your bag for them.

One of the most essential keys to any enjoyable trip is that you are able to move around freely without having to worry about luggage getting lost or broken. If you are planning for a trip that is going to be extensive, such as going to multiple countries in Europe or multiple towns in a large country of the world, you also do not want to have to lug around a heavy bag that would soon become an exhausting endeavor. Yes, travelling light is one of the keys to maintaining a comfortable and fluid travelling lifestyle. In the world of backpacking, one of the measures of a really good traveler is how light his or her bag is when travelling.

These are the same principles that experienced hikers live by while on the path. You may even incorporate a hike or trek in as a part of your trip, so similar correlations can be made between the two. Moving about is intrinsic to the definition of travelling, so a good way to go about planning what you will pack is to put yourself in the mentality that you will be carrying this stuff around with you quite a bit. You will want to prioritize your items in an order of easy accessibility when you pack based on the frequency that you will be using them and how quickly you may need to get a hold of them. In addition to that, aiming to carry items that are lighter in weight, more compact and more slender also become something important to consider.

You would not want to have to dig through your clothes that may even be dirty every time you go looking for a snack or your camera in the middle of the day. You would also not want to have to stop on a hike or venture through a large city every 20 minutes because your bag is too heavy or the weight of it is causing the straps to cut into your shoulders. Then there is the matter of also taking into consideration extra baggage fees when travelling by plane.

Reasons to Travel Light

- A small bag can easily fit into the overhead cabin of a plane (this means there is no need to waste time checking in luggage and waiting for it to come out on the baggage terminal, or risk having your undercarriage luggage get lost by baggage handlers or during plane transfers).
- Travelling light helps you be mobile all the time. This is perfect for any last minute change of plans or spontaneous decision to go exploring the area.

- When riding on a train in a faraway land, you can closely keep an eye on your smaller bag since you can put it on your lap or on a shelf directly above your head.

- When it is 36 degrees Celsius outside (or about 97 degrees Fahrenheit), the last thing you want is something heavy and cumbersome to be carrying around.

- When your backpacking trip involves hiking, you will want a lighter bag to take to the mountain top.

- With a lighter or smaller bag, you are more likely to be in control of your trip. This is in regard to transport on the plane and keeping track of your belongings while walking around in the streets of largely populated areas.

- Carrying bigger bags may not exactly send a positive message when you are crossing borders, depending on where you are travelling to. Border patrol guards could give themselves reason to be suspicious and want to search your bags, which will disturb your nice packing job but more importantly, taking important time away from your day.

- Are you uncomfortable leaving your bag at the hostel? No problem, you can take it with you anytime and anywhere!
- You will have more room for souvenir items – yahoo!!!

Stick to ONE Bag – No If's, No But's

When aiming to travel light, you should always impose one golden rule upon yourself that all backpackers know: 'Thou shalt bring no more than one travelling bag'. After all, that is the essence of real backpacking.

Many experts would recommend bringing a bag that weighs 12 kilograms (or roughly 25lbs) once it is filled. However, if you can really not resist taking that extra pair of jeans or a small cosmetic kit, just make sure that your bag does not weigh more than 30% of your actual body weight.

Now, here is the fun part – the *'how on earth am I going to fit everything in my bag'* part of the process. To start off, make a list of all the things you want to bring and start narrowing them down. Once you have settled upon your essentials, it is definitely a good idea to keep your revised list with you on your trip of everything that you are taking. This will help you keep track of all your belongings as you travel. Depending on the extent of your trip, you will be going through the process of packing and unpacking several times from place to place. Keeping such a list with you will help to make sure that you have not forgotten anything. You will want to store it in a protected place with your other important documents such as a record of your vaccinations and photocopies of your passport. To help you with developing a solid packing list, take a look over the following rules of the thumb:

- Find the right bag. Do not just grab an old school backpack. Go for real travel backpacks that open like a suitcase. Check also to make sure that the suspension system (shoulder straps) of your backpack of choice offers the comfort you need for long walks and runs.

  These will often be ones that are wide with extra padding on the straps that is made with a breathable material to wick sweat so that you will not develop heat or friction rash. The straps should also offer enough length for a comfortable adjustment and some kind of secure mechanism on the ends so that they do not slip through the buckle.

Good travel backpacks should also have two different carry-on handles; one on top, and another one on the sides somewhere. Sizes also matters. Check if your backpack can be expanded or folded.

The best backpacks are hiker's bags that range in size from 150 to 230 liters or roughly 40 to 60 gallons. They are tube-shaped so that they fit along the length of your back to distribute the weight of the bag evenly. Many come with a basic frame sewn into the part of the bag that goes against your back along with more padding so it is a comfortable fit with extra support. There are many different kinds of bags like these with all different kinds of bells and whistles on them. Of course you will want to travel in style, so pick the one that speaks to you.

Some standards to take into consideration when choosing the right pack are double stitching along the seams and a lightweight but durable material. You do not want the bag to tear or fall apart on you while you are on your trip. Other things to think about are outside pockets on the bag so that you have easier access to items you need readily available like your toothbrush, a camera, pocketknife and so on. Just know that the way the outside pockets are designed with the rest of the bag matter while you are packing the inside of your bag, You will want the outside pockets to be designed with room to expand or protrude out a little from the body of the bag. Some bags have exterior pockets sewn flush with the body so that once you have filled the bag, there is little room left to put anything in your exterior pockets, or you must compromise your fingers while trying to get the items out.

Other than that, you may be asking about room for a sleeping bag or mat, or a water bottle? Several types of bags come equipped with extra loops and bungee cords sewn onto the exterior for just such things. Shopping for the right bag can be a fun and personal experience for it will become a part of you while you travel, so take your time in choosing the one you like best that suits all of your needs.

- Bring personal wear in three's. Yes, series of three are significant and many things come in three's so let's apply the same concept here. Whether you are bound to go for a three week hike or a three month backpacking trip, carrying three pairs of underwear, socks, and shirts should be sufficient. You can wear one while the other is being washed and dried and another one will be ready to be worn next. It is a funny exception when it comes to wardrobe patterns, but somehow shorts and pants seem to be able to make the extra stride that other articles of clothing cannot. So you can change up the rule of three by bringing two pairs of shorts and a pair of jeans or cargo pants instead.

- Take your sarong and forget everything. Well, not everything, but once you have your sarong with you, you will also have an instant blanket, towel, sunshade, scarf and even a skirt. What is this mystical article? Well, if you do not know or you have not figured it out from its listed uses, it is a rectangular-shaped, thin, flowing material that can be made from different types of fabrics and serves as a multi-purpose garment for all occasions.

- Ask yourself, "Will I actually be using that? Really?" Many people sometimes get held up in the packing process thinking that they may be bringing too little. That is the idea, actually. If you do not need it, then do not bring it. There is no need to take your portable game console, an extra pair of shoes and three pairs of sunglasses. Although you may dislike reading it, leave your blow dryer behind too.

Many people possess the power of reasoning to convince themselves that they *need* to bring certain things that are usually not necessary. Here is an exercise to test that skill and get you really thinking about proper item packing: If you can come up with several scenarios where you can make practical use of an item while on your trip and highlight those uses as being necessary to the overall experience, then you may stand to take it with you. Remember that you are going on a trip; you are not leaving your whole way of life behind for good, so you can always come back to these things later.

- Remind yourself that you no longer live in the Jurassic era. You are likely to find soap, toothpaste, and shampoo even in the remotest of all areas. You do not have to bring a half-liter sized bottle of shampoo and conditioner along with you, but it does not hurt to take a small, travel-size bathroom kit with you as well. Bar soap is bulky, liquid bath soap tends to last longer. If you are keen and intent on bringing body lotion, travel size will make it much easier to carry around as well. Bring a few plastic bags to keep them in so that they do not spill. You can use your hands instead of a loofa or washcloth, but these items do not take entirely too much space so bring them if you feel it necessary.

Otherwise if you are comfortable with options, go for soap when you get there.

- Thank God for smartphones, right? You will not need to take a map, pen, compass, game consoles, laptops, or cameras with you because those slick devices have it all rolled into one. Everything can be done with a few clicks here and there. That being said, they can also be a blessing and a burden. Having such quick access to vast amounts of information at your fingertips can create a dependency that may actually take away from potential experiences in your immediate vicinity. It is really just a matter of discretion. If you are looking at your smartphone every chance you get, you will be missing out on all the real life stimulation that is all around you.

A couple of examples of scenarios where it may be better to tap into your immediate environment rather than the digital interface you carry in your hand are as follows. When you have a packed schedule it is always easier to make a quick reference to your phone for directions. However, if you have some time to wander about, why not ask some of the locals about good places to go? This will give you some interaction time and a chance to experiment with making yourself open to the unexpected opportunities that can arise out of these genuine interactions, such as finding a secluded garden in the city, a quaint restaurant or pub that most locals only know about, or meeting with new people that can lead to a whole new adventure in your day.

Rather than consulting your phone for direct information, asking around can lead to gaining insights about your immediate area that you would have otherwise not known about. It can spark conversations with local people that will add to and enrich your day, as well as help you get to know more about the culture of the people there by the way that they express themselves and the things that they talk about. Furthermore, you will be developing personal skills to be able to better rely on yourself as a traveler rather than depending so much on the device. As I said, it is simply a matter of discretion. The idea here is to develop and create organic interactions while you travel to get the most out of your experience.

The Master Checklist for Backpacking

When it comes to being a master packer and creating the ultimate preparation kit for your travels, you will want to take a look at the kinds of demands from the place or places you will be travelling to in order to help guide the decision making process. What season are you travelling in? What is the typical climate of the place that you are going to this time of year? It is a really good idea to research your destination and perhaps even get a few reviews from people who have been there to get a better sense of what to prepare for such as mosquito prevalence, local water quality, and lack of peanut butter. Seriously, if you are a fan, it does not exist in some parts of the world so you may want to bring your own.

If you are planning to go to Thailand, India, or a coastal region, it will obviously be very hot, but you will want to be prepared with a long-sleeved shirt or over shirt and a light jacket. It is very possible to experience cold nights, especially near the beach and more arid places like New Delhi and Japur in India. Even though the days may be hot, if you are staying in a coastal region, winds coming off of the water can make for a very chilly night. An extra garment for warmer weather will also come in handy when backpacking through mountainous regions, climbing at higher altitudes.

If you still find it a bit tough to work out your own backpacking list then you can always resort to the one below. The list is divided into two parts: documents and everyday essentials.

Document Items

☐ Passport and at least two photocopies - never go anywhere without these close to you. Leave at least one photocopy in your wallet and another one in your bag.

☐ Travel insurance - this is highly recommended. Never cross any border or leave your country without it. Disasters may happen and it is never a bad idea to prepare for it.

☐ Visas – the regulations and requirements for visas differ from country to country depending on where you go as well as what country your passport says you are from. It could be that you do not need to obtain a visa at all if your specific country's passport allows you an automatic tourist visa in the country you are travelling to for a given amount of time. In other cases, there are very strict regulations that require you to apply for one well in advance of your trip.

Do the necessary research to find out where you stand when it comes to visa requirements. Also, you will want to apply for a visa, if you are required to, early on in the planning stages of your trip. It is a very arduous and sensitive bureaucratic process that can sometimes take months from the time you send your passport away with the visa application to the time you actually get it back with the visa stamped inside it.

Make a few photocopies of your visa(s) and keep them along with your passport photocopies.

☐ Credit cards that allow cash withdrawals abroad – bring at least two. You can use one as a backup.

☐ Debit cards

☐ Proof of vaccinations – it will be smart to have a couple photocopies of these also.

☐ e-tickets / booking confirmation – getting boarding passes online and printing them out before you reach the airport is always the best way to go. There are also kiosks in airports near the check-in areas for many air carriers where you can print your boarding pass out if you have booked your ticket online. Most of the time it will save you having to wait in line at the check-in desk if you have managed to pack your bag to an efficient size that will allow you to carry it onboard the plane.

☐ List of all the items you have packed

☐ Driver's license / personal and international if you have one – even if you are not planning to drive in the country you are travelling, it is always good to have these on you in cases of emergency that require additional identification.

Everyday Essentials

- ☐ Flip-flops or sandals
- ☐ Walking trainers – if you are planning on doing a lot of walking, it may be in your benefit to purchase a pair of rubber or gel insoles to put in your shoes for added comfort.
- ☐ Underwear (3 pairs)
- ☐ Travel toothbrush with small tube of toothpaste
- ☐ Small bar of soap or small bottle of liquid bath soap and a travel size bottle of shampoo
- ☐ Socks (3 pairs)
- ☐ Wool socks (2 pairs – if you ever go to colder places)
- ☐ 2 pairs of trousers / cargo shorts/ fisherman shorts
- ☐ A pair of jeans or pants made from another type of durable material such as a poly blend
- ☐ 1 swimsuit
- ☐ 1 towel – do your best to pack a towel that is not too big or thick so that you can save space in your bag
- ☐ Shirts (3 pieces)
- ☐ 2 long-sleeve tops
- ☐ 2 bandanas
- ☐ 1 sarong

☐ 1 waterproof jacket – you can also just bring a comfortable jacket that will keep you warm in times of need and bring a poncho in case of rainy weather.

☐ 1 hat (preferably with a wide brim) to add some shade to your face and protect your head from the blazing sun.

☐ A pair of sunglasses

☐ Extra zip locked bags – whether you have a small case for your toiletry items or not, it is a good idea to put them in these bags, as well as putting snacks in separate bags, to avoid messes.

☐ Your iPod/mp3 player for entertainment

☐ Outlet adaptors for the country you will be in – outlet plugs are not universal! There are roughly six different types of outlet shapes around the world, and you can find outlet adaptor kits at commercial retail stores or online to accommodate charging your electronic devices in other countries.

Some Packing Tricks You Should Know

Rolling

This is ideal for stretchy fabrics that do not wrinkle whether it is a shirt, a sweater, pants, or jeans. Rolling is also the most effective space saver especially when you are using an unstructured bag such as backpack or a hiker's bag.

For pants, simply fold them lengthwise. The back pockets should be facing outward. Start rolling them from the cuffs up to the waistband. Do this as tightly as possible. Think of it like rolling up a sleeping bag. For shirts, fold each shirt lengthwise and tuck the sleeves in. Start folding from top to bottom. Do the same for jackets, but make sure that you zip it all the way down. Try to squeeze out as much air as possible. Do this for all articles of fabric including your bandanas, sarong, towel and swimsuit.

Prioritizing Your Packing Order

You will want to prioritize how you put your items into your bag so you do not have to go rummaging deeply through it anytime you need something out of there. Start by packing your jacket and a day's worth of clothing at the bottom to create a nice cushioned layer for any electronic devices you may be packing like a laptop or tablet. Put these devices in next, laying them lengthwise on end and against the side of the bag that will be resting on your back. That way you can assure that they will be well-protected. Also, you will know right where it is with a relative ease of access for when you have to take it out at the airport security check. Lay your sandals or flip-flops on end the same way you did as your laptop or tablet and against these devices. Put your trainers standing up on the toe-end opposite your flip-flops. They will slip out of your bag more easily in this orientation. Next you can put the rest of your rolled-up clothing in the bag between the flip-flops and shoes at the outer layer of the bag. Keep your hat, bandanas, and sarong near the top because you never know when you may need these.

Now it is time to fill in the rest of your bag with all the little miscellaneous things. If you brought a toiletry bag you can put that in the bag on top of all your other things along with your hat. If you just brought a toothbrush and toothpaste and plan to get the rest of the items like shampoo and such when you arrive, you can put those things in the exterior pockets of your bag. The same goes for your music player, sunglasses, snacks, pocketknife, camera, maps and compass if you choose to bring them and a travel journal and pens if you would like to bring these things too.

Some backpacks have an extra compartment in the top flap for larger miscellaneous items like a hard case for your device chargers and earphones or a book. Some also have a zipper at the bottom of the bag so that you have an extra compartment with a drawstring cord on the inside to keep all of your other belongings from falling out. This extra bottom compartment is an excellent place to keep your dirty clothes. If your bag does not have one of these, it is always best to keep your dirty clothes at the bottom of the bag anyways so they do not get in the way. Keep them sealed away in a smaller bag so they do not stink up the rest of your belongings. You should have also found a backpack that will allow you to attach or secure a small sleeping bag on the bottom or the front of it. And you are set to go! Whenever, wherever, whatever you do, your backpack is now prepared for easy, convenient and comfortable travel.

Of course you do not have to do it exactly this way, but from this illustration hopefully you will get the idea that you should put your least used items in the most inaccessible places while you put your most used items in the most accessible places. Account for devices that will have to be removed at security checkpoints when travelling so that you can take them out and put them back in your bag easily enough without having to disturb the rest of your contents. Keep small items in small compartments so that they do not get lost easily. When you develop a system to keep your bag organized, you will not have to spend so much time with it throughout your trip and can place your attention on more important things like where you can find some entertainment for the evening.

Other Packing Hacks to Know

- Use any hard case you have (e.g. old sunglasses case) to store your electronic device chargers and earphones. This will keep them untangled and easy to locate.

- Use an old ID lanyard for your whistle, keys, and for securing your small handheld camera.

- Always put your liquid items in zip lock bags to avoid potential spilling disasters and problems with airport regulations.

- Always bring a cloth laundry bag or durable plastic bag with you to keep your dirty clothes out of contact with your clean clothes.

- Shoe cases are bulky, so you may want to use a disposable shower cap to wrap your footwear instead.

- Keep a parachute cord bracelet handy. These are also widely known as paracord bracelets. You can find them online, at craft and outdoors stores, and most army/navy stores. They can be used them to tie your things up, to use as an instant clothesline and for any emergency purpose too. They do not always come with instructions on how to tie them back up neatly into a bracelet, but the process is simple once you learn the steps, so a quick search online will show you how.

- If you cannot travel without your razor, make sure that you protect the blade by using a big clip/binder.

- Lock your backpack/baggage when using transport over long distances. Many people are keen to buy some sort of locks for the zippers of their backpacks or bags when traveling, especially by plane where they may not always be with their bag if it is checked in. If you just happen to be one of these people or were not aware of it before but now think it is a good idea, well congratulations! It is a good idea! However, there are the right locks to use and there are the wrong ones. The wrong ones will be cut open by airport security so that they can check through your bag if they need to for security reasons. Then you will have wasted money and the locks will have served no purpose. The right locks are ones approved by TSA – Transportation Security Administration – and will say so right on the package if and when you purchase them.

Another option to consider when it comes to securing your baggage is to use plastic zip ties at the zippers instead. They are quite cheap to buy, and if airport security happens to cut them in a security check, you can carry some with you and just slip another one back on your bag.

Chapter 3

It Is All About The Money

Isn't it the truth? Let's face it – you cannot go anywhere without a bit of cash in your pocket. Travel is never free. The moment you step out of the door, you know that you will be needing money to get through the day. In travelling, money is your primary requirement. Jessie J got it right --- in the world of travelling, it is all about the money!

For many travelers or aspiring travelers, money tends to be the biggest roadblock. This particularly hurdles the younger travelers – those who have not really started saving yet. Looking at the travel brochures and meeting people who have been abroad quite a few times can be very enticing. So should you halt your dream of travelling then? The answer is NOT AT ALL.

Do not let money stand in the way of your greatest travelling desires! Sure it will cost some to get started. The whole point of travelling light and going off of the beaten, glitzed up path is that you can still have the pleasurable experience of travel without having to pay dearly for it. This is perhaps a lesson that can be taken from youth and young travelers then: it may be true that they have less experience and vaguer concepts of money management in larger sums, although the bare truth is that they still find ways to make things happen for themselves, perhaps even because they are used to not having money.

Successful young travelers will be told many times, "That is good that you are travelling. Get it in while you are young!" There may be many reasons why they hear this particular expression. Ultimately it may be that with time, although the desire to travel and experience some exciting mystery and freedom does not leave a person entirely, the idea of it becomes too big to handle.

So many of us are conditioned to an idea of costly expenses when it comes to travelling without really knowing why sometimes they are that way and other times there are various ways to go about it. When you read from this book that the backpacking world has been changing over the last few decades, that specific notion is what it is talking about. More and more people are realizing that they can get creative with ways to cut expenses and still have a good time.

Travelling can get less expensive, too, if you only exert a bit of an effort researching how you are going to do it. In this book, you are going to obtain the tricks on how you can still devour the pleasure of travelling without breaking your bank! To do this, you have to get drenched in the perspective of a real backpacker and not that of a glampacker. *Do you still remember the difference?* So if you are ready, here is a quick rundown on how you can fulfill your dream of backpacking without getting bankrupt.

Three Basic Rules for Cost-Efficient Backpacking Trips

Rule 1. Prepare, prepare, and prepare.

As cliché as it may sound, in order to maximize the chances of exploring abroad and get the most out of your trip, the best way is by getting financially ready. Take at least eight months to a year to prepare for your backpacking trip and start putting away for it little by little. This will give you ample time to set aside a fraction of your salary or allowance before heading out of the country. Make sure that you save this money on a separate account so you do not mix your emergency, retirement, mortgage money and so on with your travelling budget.

Once you have your destination in mind, creating a budget for it will help turn the idea into a well-defined, clarified vision and bring you that much closer to making it happen. Begin looking up the cost of plane tickets to get a working notion of how much you will be shooting for. There are few helpful tips to know when it comes to buying plane tickets; you can call them traveler's secrets.

To get the best price, it will help to start looking about eight months our before you plan to leave. Keep checking the prices every week to develop an eye for trends. Flight ticket prices fluctuate like the stock market. Buying your ticket about three months before your flight date is usually when they are the cheapest. Flying on a Tuesday or Wednesday is always cheaper, whereas flying on the weekends is always the most expensive time of the week to travel. Around the holidays is when airports see the highest volume of travelers, and when demand is up, so go the prices. Therefore if you can manage to plan for a flight about a week or two after a holiday when everyone has returned back home, you may find that ticket prices have dipped as well.

For some reason, it usually goes that looking for plane tickets in the following year is always more expensive than the current year until about November or so. This is why it is recommended to keep an eye on the prices well in advance of even seriously considering purchasing your tickets, as the year-end wrap rule is not always a consistent one. Try to make the parameters of your flight details as open as possible: if you keep the search options open to 'any time' and 'search for nearby airports,' you will increase your chances of finding lower prices. Although it goes to say that flying to and from major airport hubs is often cheaper, play around with searching your destination airport. You may find that not only can you get a more affordable ticket, but it could land you in an area you had not thought of to explore that might offer you the opportunity for a starter side adventure before getting to your central place of choice. Ground transportation by train or bus is cheap in most places around the world anyways. It is also true that taking a multiple flight option to reach your destination will afford you lower end ticket rates rather than a direct, non-stop flight. Just be sure to make a note of the delay times in between flights. Sometimes the compromise of time is not worth the savings, say like spending 14 hours in an airport between flights.

By creating a spreadsheet or recorded budget of all the items that you will need on your trip such as the plane ticket, accommodation costs, food, ground transport, alcohol beverages, attractions and souvenirs, you will have a much more solid idea of what you will be saving for and a realistic plan of what your daily budget will be. As you go along doing research in your planning stage, you will get a better feeling for knowing what your experience will look like and you can just slide prices right into the slots on your spreadsheet.

To jazz up your experience abroad a bit and perhaps create a highlighted center that all of the other events you will be taking in can revolve around, you may want to look into an activity that your area of choice is well-known for or one that it specializes in. For example if you go to a South American country you may want to look into the time of year where they have 'Ferias' or carnival festivals that are brightly colored and high in energy. You may also like to spring some extra money for an authentic Thai massage or Ayurvedic massage in India. It is always best to throw at least an extra couple hundred dollars on top your finalized travel budget too; you will want to err on the side of over budgeting to be safe and better prepared.

This is very important and many people often disappoint themselves after unintentionally spending their other savings money during the backpacking trip. Be reasonable and be a responsible spender. You can always keep a large save jar in your house for your loose change and small bills or any money you can spare for your trip. You can make it a game such as every time you see something during your day or online that reminds you of your trip you have to put some contribution to your fund. This will help build your savings on a consistent basis as well as keep you motivated to make the trip happen. You will also appreciate the work you are putting in to make this dream of yours a reality.

Rule 2. Choose a developing country over a developed one.

Sure, the Eiffel tower and the Big Ben clock sound just like anyone's dream destinations and these can be yours if you do have the money to see them. Although it is not exactly a bad idea to dream of Europe, you may want to explore the less travelled road too. Choosing developing countries over developed ones is not always a question of money. For many, this could also be about self-discovery. Why make plans for a destination that everyone has heard of when you can travel to somewhere seldom mentioned, even to your own awareness?

Experiencing a world and a culture that may be unexpected can offer you the promise of a greater adventure and learning experience. You will be reaching into a realm that will defy your expectations no matter what your style of travel may be. When you do not have standardized expectations for a certain place with regard to, "Oh, I have seen that in a movie," or, "I have heard that people typically live like that in that place," you allow for a much more vivid engagement to appeal to all of your senses and create a more impressionable and memorable trip. You will be coming back with memories of a story that is all your own, unfettered from dulled, jaded or mainstream third party references.

There can be a happy medium between the expensive, overly exotic and commonly touristic destinations. Every place in the world has this appealing middle ground, and often times while people are trying so hard to get an authentic experience in popular places while staying out of the tourist traps, the genuine spark they are looking for is just around the corner and down an unsuspecting side street or just in the next town over. The best advice I have ever read and actually did by my own nature before reading it came from a Frommer's guide to travelling book. It read that one way to really get to know a place and find certain hidden treasures that it has to offer is to safely and unsuspiciously follow a local around for a bit. Yes, I know what you are thinking, it may sound dubious at first. If you are willing to try it though, it is possible that they may lead you down a hidden side street that contains quaint and wondrous shops or a restaurant or pub teeming with spirited local life.

Rule 3. Manage your expectations.

Again, you are backpacking and not going on a grand vacation, although with the right attitude you can make them one in the same. You may find yourself on some days 'surfing couches' or staying in a non-air-conditioned room. That should not bother you at all. When backpacking, you are leaving a little comfort behind in exchange for a life-enriching experience. It serves to provide you with great grounding sustenance amidst feeling like you are flying on the thrills of wanderlust. Those flu shots you needed to take prior to taking off will all be worth it.

Top 10 Budget Destinations that Will WOW Your Eyes and Your Pockets

- **Thailand.** Are you wondering why Europeans are starting to flock to this country? Well, aside from the glorious beaches and good food, this Asian country is also becoming the new mecca for travelers on the oriental side of the planet. Young backpackers from France, Germany and other parts of Europe are now choosing Thailand as one of the most viable options due to the inexpensive way of life. Of course, this does not include all the tourists taking a plunge in the Krabi or Phuket beaches or the tourists and shoppers in Bangkok.

  Heading north of Thailand is now becoming a target destination of tourists on a tight budget. To get to one of the majestic regions known as Chang Mai, an overnight train can be taken for a mere $12. In this region, you may also find rooms to rent for a low as $3 per night. The key is to manage your expectations. For these $3 rooms, you can find something clean and somewhat comfortable. If you are worried that you may be wandering in a not-so-interesting place, well put your concerns away because Chang Mai's rich flora and fauna may just be the reason for you to come back again someday.

- **Cambodia.** Exploring Ankor Wat in Seam Riep maybe one of the most exhilarating adventures that any backpacker exploring Southeast Asia could experience. On top of this, it may also be one of the cheapest stops. There are rooms that can be rented for a mere $3-5 per night. The transport systems and food are also among the cheapest in the entire region. Aside from the world-famous Ankor Wat temple, backpackers can also take a break on the beaches of Sihanouksvile or Koh Rong. These stunning beaches can be accessed via a boat ride for $5 per person.

- **Indonesia.** Not too far from Thailand, this other favorite destination is often mistaken for a very expensive place to visit. If you stay on the beautiful and high-end beach resorts in Bali, then you may find yourself splurging a lot of money. However, there are neighboring towns that can offer you the same adventure but at a fraction of the amount. For instance, you can find $10-per-night rooms at Ubud which would be more than sufficient for any backpacker.

Moreover, traveling in Bali for just a $25-a-day budget is possible. As an example, food in this country is relatively cheap. Buffet meals can range around $3 while a plate of their traditional *nasi goreng* can be bought for less than $2. You can also snack on their local spring rolls for just $0.50. However, if you start missing Western food, restaurants are available in key areas and you can take advantage of these foods for about $5 to $10.

- **India.** When cultural exploration is your prime reason for backpacking, then you should not leave India off your list. The country overflows with cultural richness – the languages, the festivities, the people, the food, the sights, the colors – you name it and India can certainly give your eyes and your heart the pleasures they need. Many backpackers in India have attested to surviving on a $15 to $20-a-day budget. Your food budget may range from $ 0.70 to $2 per meal, whereas a decent room can be rented for $15 a night. Transportation is quite cheap, too. However, it is important to know that tipping is customary in India. Everyone is expected to offer a little 'backsheesh' even just for simplest things.

Aside from seeing the Taj Mahal, the floating palace of Jaipur and the holy place called Varanasi, going on a camel safari is highly recommended. Taking a sip of India tea called Chai along the street is also a favorite activity of many backpackers.

- **The Philippines.** The beaches, the sounds, the street foods, and the smiles – these are just among the top reasons why backpackers never fail to hit the islands of the Philippines. The reasonably priced accommodations and the cheap yet superb beer can certainly give any traveler the boost they need.

Going to renowned beaches like Boracay offers travelers a range of options; from cheap accommodations and reasonably priced foods, to the most expensive. For backpackers, finding a room for $20 to $25 a night is a piece of cake, even on the popular island of Boracay. Buffet meals along the beach are offered for $5 to $10 per person. Ice-cold beers are also available for merely $3.

There is also a plethora of activities that can be done on the island for free: snorkeling, making sand castles, sunset watching, jogging, walking along the 4-km beach, and of course, basking under the sun. However, if you do have a few dollars to spare you can go parasailing, helmet scuba diving, and island-hopping.

- **Nicaragua.** The country may have suffered from political unrest, but it is now welcoming tourists from across the globe. Nicaragua is also hailed as one of the most budget-friendly destinations in the entire Central

America. The prices in this country are now comparable to those in Southeast Asia. For example, one can easily find a room to rent for a mere $5 a night in the colonial city called Granada. Even in the top tourist destination known as San Juan Del Sur, cheap accommodations of about $10 a night can be found. A typical bean and rice Nicaraguan dish can be enjoyed for only $4 per meal. Before you leave Nicaragua, make sure that you check its majestic volcanic lake called Laguna de Apoyo. It is located just 20 minutes from Granada.

- **Bolivia.** If Southern America has been enticing you for years but your budget falls short of being able to afford to see the wonders of Brazil or Argentina, you may opt to visit Bolivia first. The cheapest accommodations can range between $5 to $7 a night. However, hostels are also available and you can rent a bed for a reasonable $10 per night. Guest houses are also available if you are travelling in groups of 3 to 5 people which could cost roughly $8 a head.

- **Costa Rica.** If you are not yet ready to leave the Americas, then you should give Costa Rica a quick visit.

There is a lot to see: volcanoes, beaches, lakes, national parks, and wildlife. As most of these activities are only for sightseeing, you do not need to pay a huge sum of money. A visit to the Corcovado National Park or Palo Verde National Park may be one of the first things you would like to do. You can even set up camp in certain spots. Better yet, you can rent out rooms for only $10 per night. Costa Rican food can also range from $ 3 to $5 a meal. A daily budget of $30 to $35 should be sufficient.

- **Turkey.** There is so much to see in Turkey. The blending between Asian and European influences makes this country a must-visit among travelers and backpackers. The iconic city of Istanbul is a good place to explore. It is the home to Hagia Sophia, the magnificent Chora Church, and the Old Istanbul. And if your feet get worn out from all the walks and exploration, you may head to the Grand Bazaar food market for good food and cheap finds. This market has over 4,000 outlets to keep you busy. You can enjoy traditional Middle Eastern foods for prices ranging from $3 to $5 and a cheap hotel accommodation for only $20 a night.

- **Albania.** This country is not typically included in most backpackers' need-to-visit list. However, this country offers a better alternative to European countries such as Greece and Italy. Albania's Mediterranean views also offer tourists a feel of Europe, but at a much more reasonable price. The capital, Tirana, is a good place to explore even when on a tight budget. The museums and historical monuments can be viewed for free just like when you opt for a hike at Mount Dajti. Backpackers who love the beach life may give the Jala Beach a visit. All of these can be done on a tight budget of $25 a day.

When in Europe: Money Saving Tips and Tricks

Europe will always be a person's dream destination. Although exploring this relatively borderless continent requires money, it is good to know that you can actually fulfill your dream of a European tour without spending too much.

How to save on accommodations

1. Booking online is good, but for the low season you may want to book directly with the hostel of your choice. During the off-peak period it is more likely that you can haggle a little when booking for a room at a hostel.

The quality of hostel accommodations varies widely. Even though they are cheaper than staying at conventional hotels, some of them on the higher cost end can appear quite charming like hotels, except instead of the ritzy look they appear more cozy and homey. On the other end, you may be able to pay the equivalent of $10 per night for a place that has the feel of a college dormitory. The rooms here can be fitted with three bunk beds each.

There are usually furnished common areas which make great places to meet other travelers, stock up on recommendations for sights and attractions to go or share your own. Some hostels are connected with the local traveling community and offer their own attractions such as bike tours of the city in Amsterdam. You will find that many hostels offer up a kitchen so that you can cook your own food, but if you are counting on this then you should make sure that one is available when booking ahead.

A quick chat with the attendant at the desk will allow you to locate and securely store their baggage room where you can safely keep your belongings and access them at most any time. Be sure to talk about these times with the attendant though as well as what times to be back if you decide to stay out a bit late for the night. Some hostels will close up and lock their door entrance around 10 p.m. to 12 a.m. If you get caught outside after they have locked up, well my friend, it will be an occasion to make the most out of the night life and into the wee hours for you because most hostels with this policy are very strict about it.

2. Be informed on the cancellation policy of the hostel. For many travelers, it is common to have the first night cancelled due to various reasons: late flights,

last minute changes, etc. Make sure you understand what you are risking should you wish to cancel a night you have booked already. Some places require that you cancel within a specific timeframe. If you have booked online, some hostel websites make it mandatory that you cancel online also, otherwise you may not get your money back cancelling by phone or in person.

3. Try couch surfing. For the adventurous minds, couch surfing is a good way to save money. Instead of booking an entire hotel room during the travel, you may want to 'rent a couch' instead. It is really cheap and sometimes even free depending on whom you may find to 'rent' from. These are usually free-spirited people who have been travelers themselves and know that if hotels can be an avoided expense, a welcoming residential place, albeit a couch, is an appreciated alternative. This is also an excellent way to really interact with the locals.

One resource to get a feel for how it is done is to go to www.couchsurfing.com. Locals who have a place to offer up will have a profile page and a way to contact them so you can get somewhat acquainted with them beforehand. They are also rated by previous couch surfers who leave comments as well, giving a more assured vote of confidence for the safety of yourself and your belongings during your stay.

Though it may sound like a very lenient operation, as it often is, availability for these places can also fill up quickly depending on the travel season. So be sure to treat it the same as you would for booking a hostel or hotel room and look into it ahead of time.

4. For groups of travelers, splitting a hotel room is not a bad idea. If you are travelling with friends, you may want to book a room with multiple beds instead. This idea may come handy if you land in the expensive countries of Europe such as France, Germany and England.

5. Camping. Lucky you, there are a lot of camp sites in every part of Europe. You may want to rent a tent instead of a room. What other way to get a feel for the countryside like sleeping right in the middle of it and waking up to the natural sights and sounds of it the next day, right? This is a good way to commune with nature and to meet people along the way. You will be sure to meet other backpackers along the way with whom you can share stories and food, make friends, and perhaps learn even more travel tips and places to visit from them too.

6. For long trips, say crossing one border to another for example, taking the overnight train is advised. This is like shooting two birds with one stone – travelling and resting in one shot. You may have to rent a bed car, but it would not be as expensive as staying in a hotel.

7. Try sleeping at the airport. This can be done if your trip is scheduled at the most uncompromising hour. Instead of staying an extra night at a hotel, you can cancel it altogether and stay at the airport instead.

Remember those 14 hour delays between stops on a multi-flight ticket that were discussed earlier? This is where they actually become relevant and perhaps even worthwhile. Airports allow ticketed travelers to sleep for free. They have plenty of comfortable furniture and some airports even have specific rooms for people with long delays.

During the nighttime the volume of travelers dwindles to a trickle and by 10 or 11 p.m., even in the largest of airports, you are likely to have most of the place to yourself aside from a few other wandering souls who have found themselves in a similar situation as you. Thus said, along with the security cameras and staff, you can rest assured that you and your bag will be safe while you sleep.

How to Save on Food While Backpacking in Europe

1. Try the groceries. Instead of hitting up restaurants all the time, you may want to buy your next meal at the

grocery store next time. You can have a nice picnic somewhere. This is a great and cheap way to consistently snack throughout the day so you are not left hungry. You can eat fresh foods without having to cook too. You may also want to purchase your alcohol from the grocery store and simply consume it with friends at the hostel. Some countries allow the casual consumption of alcoholic beverages openly on the street as well. There are usually trash cans near every street corner, so you can throw them out too instead of littering.

2. Cook your own food. You may get your finest ingredients at the farmer's market, partaking in the local produce. If you are staying at a hostel, then you can cook in the kitchen instead. Pots, cookware, and utensils are usually made available by the hostel kitchen. If you are unsure, you can always ask the person at the desk. This is also a good way to make new friends. Otherwise you can look into a one-time buy or renting a cheap portable grill or hotplate.

3. Book at a hostel that offers free breakfast. By doing so, you can already be assured of one meal per day. Some hostels also offer free-flowing coffee. Put your research skills to test and you will have some success in finding these no problem.

4. Bring some snacks with you. You can stuff your bag with biscuits and some fruit, nutrition bars or fresh vegetables. You can eat while on the road.

5. Do your homework first. Find some information on cheap restaurants around the area by researching online or better yet ask some locals nearby. When you have finally made a choice, do not forget to take advantage of the lunch specials.

6. When dining at a restaurant, ask for 'table water'. You have to be specific about it because sometimes if you only ask for 'water', they might serve you an expensive bottle of sparkling water. Table water is free and is equivalent to a pitcher of potable water.

7. Try the street foods. Yes, this is part of the cultural exploration and not just about saving money. Try the local sandwiches, kebabs, sweets and other edible goodies that you may find in some larger town or city streets. It is probably wise though to make this an occasional endeavor because extensive use of this food resource will end up chipping away at your budget in nickels and dimes before you know it. Europe is the hub of epicureanism; so in short, you can never go wrong even with street foods.

8. Stick to water and grab a soda when you get back home. In Europe a can of soda can be bit a pricier that you expect it to be. Moreover, they do not normally offer ice for a not-so-cold soda. Besides that, health-wise sodas are notorious for dehydrating you while water will be just the dose you need for all the moving about you will be doing, especially if you are travelling in hotter climates.

9. For a good bottle of beer, head down to the cheap bars, also known as dives. Most hostels have their own mini

bars. You can also check with your front desk where you can easily find a cheap bar. Another trick is to have your drinks at the bar and not on the regular tables. You will find that your drinks cheaper there. Also, drinking at a patio is the 'most expensive' way of dining. Stay at the bar and break the ice with the locals.

10. Try to stay away from the tourist areas for food. Tourist areas will always be more expensive as that is exactly what they are designed to do – get money out of foreign travelers, and get as much as possible. It is an industry after all. Europe has so much to offer and you may want to discover their own hidden gems when scouring for food and drinks. Tipping is not customary in most European countries either.

How to Save on Ground Transportation

1. These boots were made for walking… We were given legs to get around, so how often do we really take advantage of that? Perhaps we would have been better

off asking for wheels instead of feet. Make your trip a true experience for yourself by finding the globetrotter within you who can get to and around in most places by standing on their own to legs; and then moving them in a forward motion. This is just what you have brought your trainers for after all. It will be a great way to incorporate or prepare for a hike as well; it is free; you will have the freedom to turn on a dime when something catches your eye and meander where you please, too.

2. Rent a bicycle. These are a great way to get around in cities and towns, visit multiple attractions in one day without feeling too exhausted, and can be very cheap to rent. Cities like Amsterdam, Brussels and Copenhagen are world-renowned for their bicycle culture. Amsterdam has several dozen shops and organizations that provide bicycle tours around the city and bikes to rent by the hour, although more common is renting by the day at about $9 and for multi-day renting you can find rates as low as $4.50 per day. You may need to pay a deposit upfront of

around $22 which you will get back when you return the bike. And yes, they come with locks.

In Copenhagen there are street bikes that are available at terminals where you can simply slip a coin into the lock slot and release the bike, ride around the city at your pleasure, then get your coin back when you return the bike to the same terminal you picked it up at or a different one of many located throughout the city. If you travel to a city where you plan to stay for longer than a week, it may be in your interest to buy a used bike to get around. You can always sell it again when you are ready to depart.

3. Avoid taxis at all costs, especially those on your wallet. Taxis can be money hogs, and many times they are explicitly so to travelers. Most countries and cities that are accustomed to a volume of tourists and travelers assume that they have loads of money to spend, otherwise why travel? But you know better.

What you may not be aware of is that taxi drivers can tend to take advantage of travelers who are unfamiliar with the area by taking an especially long way to reach your destination or taking unnecessary ways that are high traffic routes so that they can earn a higher fare. If you find yourself in a situation where you end up choosing to take a taxi, try to strike up a bargain and haggle with them a little bit before you even step into the vehicle.

4. Use the subway or metro. This is the fastest way to get around in larger cities. Most of them are well-designed to bring you to all of the important and interesting parts of the city where you can usually walk from the nearest destination stop. Some of these underground systems can get pretty sophisticated and intricate with not only color codes for individual lines but also number and letter codes, and sometimes combinations of all three. Paris is a prime example of just complicated an underground subway system can get. They even have double-decker subways here.

Be sure to obtain a detailed map of the system either online or from a pamphlet at an information kiosk on the street or near or in one of the stops. Many of the stops will make it a bit easier too by having a billboard outlining all of the paths that go throughout the city. It would not be recommended to rely solely on these though, because there is a chance that you can still get lost. A map that you can carry around with you or one on your smartphone will help to ensure that you always know where you are and where you are going.

Furthermore, many cities will offer public transport passes and tickets at discounted rates if you buy them for a series of days, a week, or up to a month, depending on your length of stay. Some of these passes will cover transportation for tram lines and buses too. You can buy individual tickets which are always cheaper by themselves as long as you are not making frequent use of this kind of transportation. If you are only going to use it once or twice in the entire day, an individual ticket may be the way to go. By going this route, it will be helpful to have your day and destinations planned out and coordinated ahead of time so as to maximize your mobility and lessen the amount of walking you do. Otherwise, a multi-trip pass will free you up to do a little more spontaneous exploring without going over budget.

5. Take a tram. Trams are aboveground versions of subways. They are a bit slower in getting around because they still have to abide street traffic protocol to some degree and usually have more stops than subways do. On the plus side, they offer large windows for you to be able to see the wonders of the city upfront. If you are just travelling to get familiar with the city, you can always get off at the next stop if you have seen something along the way that has caught your interest and you want to go check out.

Just like the subway systems though, there are transportation police that will randomly board the tram to check that each passenger is carrying a valid ticket. If they catch you without one, they can lay heavy fines on you. If you do not have any cash on you, they have no problem walking you to the nearest ATM. You will often be able to buy tickets and passes for trams at the ticket counters of major metro stops.

6. Grab a bus. Buses are usually the slowest method of transport to get around in a town or city because they have to abide all traffic laws and often frequent the most amount of stops of all your transportation options as well. Like the other modes of transportation, grab yourself a ticket or pass before you get onboard. These systems can get confusing too so find yourself a bus route map with stop times either online or at the nearest transportation hub kiosk. Keep a careful lookout for certain bus lines that travel only on the weekends versus only during the weekdays. There are some routes that go all week long but frequent stops less during the weekends. You would not want to be caught waiting for a bus that never comes!

You can also book a coach bus for traveling longer distances such as from one town to the next or even to cross borders. You can usually find these tickets for a good price and they often offer quality services. You will be comfortable enough for short distances, but anything over four hours may leave you feeling cramped and in need of a good stretch. Coach lines offer these for longer distances of course for 10 to 15 minute periods and will stop at a convenience store or some place that allows you to buy snacks if the line does not provide their own.

7. Hop on a train. Trains are a great way to travel long distances on land, whether internationally or just from one town to the next within a country. They provide comfortable seating and storage for your bags that you have easy access to. You will usually have the option to buy an aisle seat ticket or get a train car with a small room that you may share with a few other travel goers. Whenever you are feeling the need to get up and move about, you may do so at your leisure. Many trains also offer a dining car service for food and beverages, so you may want to indulge yourself in this

unique experience, although you may find the prices a bit high if your budget is strapped.

If you have planned a trip to Europe in which you would like to visit a number of different countries, you have your options open as to how to get from one place to the next. There is an airline that is called Ryan Air which offers super cheap flights for many cities in Europe, just be sure to look into the baggage fees. Then there are a few distinctive train options in which different package services are provided, the two largest organizations for which are known as EuroRail/Eurail and Rail Europe.

Doing a little research online will show you all the various options they have and prices for them. Each company offers travel access to the same 23 countries in Europe, the catch is that these passes are only available to non-European residents. For European residents there is the option of purchasing InterRail passes, however those options will not be covered in this book. Of the EuroRail and Rail Europe passes, they offer discounted prices to youths under the age of 26, whereas persons 26 years of age and over must buy an adult pass.

The passes break down as follows: A global rail pass allows you to move freely throughout these 23 countries as you please, at whatever time you want. These are for backpackers who are planning the long trip of a month to three months. While the price for a global pass for an adult may seem a bit steep – over $1000 for a one month pass – it is actually a reasonably fair price for such a value. Remember too that whether it be train, plane, or automobile, automated transportation is always going to be your biggest expense, and you can compensate for it elsewhere in your budget.

There are also select rail passes that compare at cheaper rates, however they have certain constituents that can greatly shape how you determine your travel plans. These passes need to be used within a two month period, and they can only be used between bordering countries such as Germany, Austria, and Italy or Italy, France, and Spain. There are three select pass options that are governed by number of countries you can visit and number of travel days. A travel day is deemed to be a 24 hour period, so you can take as many trains from one midnight to the next depending on how and where you want to spend your day.

The three select passes start with the cheapest at around $450 for an adult, which allows you to visit three countries within five days of travel. The next is about $650 for an adult and gives you access to four countries with eight days of travel. And then there is the most expensive select pass option at right around $1,000 for which you can visit five countries within 15 days of travel, averaging out to about three days in each country or a little bit longer time on the ones you begin and end with.

Whether you choose to go for an extended train pass or just one ticket, travelling by train is quiet, comfortable, allows you to move when you need to, offers a place to sleep if travelling overnight (which is recommended), and provides an atmosphere to get acquainted with many other international travelers. Aside from all of these benefits, you also get a panoramic view of the beautiful and lush countryside throughout Europe that never gets tiring to soak in.

Larry Fisher

Chapter 4

Busting The Fears Of Backpacking Gear

When you equate backpacking to the great outdoors, then you may find yourself saving more space in your bag for the gear you need. To many, backpacking is never complete without a hike or a trek. Ascending a few hundred meters or even kilometers could mean adding more gear to include in your list. To elevate your overall experience in backpacking, you may have to start scouring for items that are considered essential.

It is also a common misconception that having to bring all this gear means an extra bag for you to carry. In fact, if you would only become overly prudent in selecting and shopping for these items, you could find yourself with just a few additional lightweight items to squeeze in your backpack. For the newbies, it is essential to do a lot of research so you can find the best gear there is. You will want to weigh out the importance of cost versus durable quality. It often does not make sense to buy cheaply if some gear is only going to last you a couple uses, unless that is your intention of course. Some brands (usually the name leaders in the market) have taken the full functionality of gear into consideration right down to the amount of space it takes up. For the experienced backpackers, it will all boil down to how well you can bundle the items together to make them all portable.

Top and Essential Gear for Backpacking

1. Maps. Ok, so you may be saying, "I have got Google Maps on the phone so why do I need to bring a real map with me?" The answer is for emergency purposes and for easy navigation. Although the Google app can be particularly useful when getting to the first point of destination, wandering through treks is completely different. Make sure that you bring the right map.

Strap it on the side of your bag so you can immediately pull it out. You may also want to keep it wrapped up in a plastic sleeve or bag to weatherproof it from rain as well as protect it from liquid spills or leaks.

2. Compass and whistle. Although these two may sound very basic or perhaps even unnecessary, many mountaineers and backpackers tend to underestimate their value and practical function. If you have the extra dough, you may also purchase a hand-held GPS system for better navigation. It is, however, not a requirement. Knowing how to use a compass can come in handy whether you are hiking or simply wandering around. It will help you to quickly orient yourself when looking at a map also. Do not forget to strap them on your pants or wear them around your neck using an old ID lanyard.

3. Sleeping bags. There are now ultra-light sleeping bags that you can carry around during your backpacking or trekking trips. Look for those sleeping bags that come with stretchy stitches so you can move around freely

without having to feel like you are being prepared for mummification. Moreover, look for a sleeping bag that can be used in all seasons. You will want to mentally put yourself in the circumstances you will be facing as best you can because there are a variety of options to consider. Weighing the pros and cons of a perfect sleeping bag for you may come down to better insulation for colder temperatures at the expense of being heavier. Or will you choose to go for a lighter one and wear more clothing layers? You will also want to take into account that like so many other products, name brands tend to be pricier but also come at a better quality. Do your research to find the best fit for you. You might be surprised how much these bags have evolved over the years.

4. Water-repellent and insect-repellent jackets. This is another backpacking breakthrough that is just worth saving your money for. These jackets do not protect you from getting drenched in the rain but they can repel all malaria and dengue-carrying mosquitos. Even if you have already been vaccinated, it would not

be such a bad idea to keep yourself even more protected. Best of all, these are lightweight too.

5. The right trail runner shoes. When backpacking, your feet do the most work. This means that you can never overlook the benefits of wearing the right trail runners. Find the pair that is not too stiff or too heavy. Water resistance is also an important criterion. Remember also from the master pack list chapter that considering how much walking and hiking you plan on doing, it might be a good idea to invest in some comfortable gel insoles like Dr. Scholl's for added support on your feet.

6. Portable cooker. Of course, you will have to eat, too, whether you are on a mountain or just camping out somewhere. A two-burner cooker or flamethrower is highly recommended. A portable grill stove can help, too, as you would no longer need to bring an extra skillet. Look at options for where you are traveling to and consider buying this item once you get over to your destination. Depending on the area, you may be

able to get it cheaper and you can always ditch it, donate it, or try to pawn it quickly when you are getting ready to leave.

7. Medicine kit. Never leave your home without this. Getting sick on the road is the biggest bummer so make sure that you have your pain killer and first-aid kit handy! Also, this will save you a lot of time from asking anyone for medicine or the nearest pharmacy.

8. Sunscreen and mosquito repellant. This is not purely vanity, but for health purposes too. You may want to refill a small plastic bottle of sunscreen or anti-mosquito solution. If you can manage it considering your options, it may be better to simply buy these once you get to your destination. Some places do not offer higher SPFs than 30, so if you have highly sensitive skin then go ahead and bring your own with you.

9. Pocketknife. The smallest or lightest pocket knife is highly recommended for backpacking. Although the

purpose is self-explanatory, it is still important to put emphasis on how helpful having one with you is during backpacking.

10. Durable drinking bottle and a torch. A strap-on bottle is highly important. A water bottle that can hold up a minimum of 1 liter is advised. If you are going to be camping in remote areas without easy access to potable water, investing in a UV light pen water purifier or a gravity fed filter will allow you to drink safely straight from any stream, river, lake or pond. Running water is always the safest. Aside from your drinking bottle, buying a camel pack is not a bad investment either. Wearing a torch or flashlight in the form of bracelet or necklace is also highly recommended. Bring extra batteries with you and store them in the small hard case where you keep your headphones and such.

Larry Fisher

Tech Stuff List for an Awesome Backpacking Experience

Aside from the fundamentals, we cannot ignore the importance of technology in making any travel experience more memorable. For many people, carrying an extra camera apart from the one of the smartphone is an absolute must. Here is an example of a list of tech stuff that you may want to carry with you on your next backpacking trip:

☐ A laptop/notebook/tablet (can be used for updating blogs, reaching out to friends, for Instagram posts, etc.)

☐DSLR Camera and an 18-135 mm lens

☐ A smartphone

☐ A spare camera battery

☐ A small and lightweight tripod with a bag

☐ A selfie stick

☐ A headphone splitter

☐ 2 flash drives

☐ 2 chargers – keep one as a back up

☐ 1 external hard drive for all the charging needs

☐ Power bank – these are portable chargers that do not require you to find an outlet for your devices low on juice.

□ Outlet adaptor for your devices and the country or region that you will be travelling through

Renting vs. Buying Backpacking Gear

For travelers, cost will always be a very important factor to implement in the planning and actual travelling stages. This is particularly true for first timers. If backpacking involves camping out or hiking, which among the items above should be bought? Is it reasonable to rent some of them instead? How can you save for the important ones? These are just few of the dilemmas for an aspiring backpacker.

For newbies, it is certainly okay to rent some of the items first if you do not want spend so much. This is understandable as you may be more focused on purchasing big items such as plane tickets and saving for the daily expenses. Not to mention, visa processing and vaccinations can be costly as well. To help you out even more, we have here a list of advantages that you may experience when renting your backpacking equipment:

- You will be able to test them before you buy one for yourself. You can see whether the brand of sleeping bag is comfortable enough. You may also check to see if the tent is spacious enough for you and your stuff. You can also experience first-hand if the portable cooker is easy to use or not. Next time, you will already have a clue as to which items you should purchase or save for.

- You can also have a range of items to choose from. When searching for items to rent, you can start by finding them online or by going to rental shops directly. You will find yourself in a room with vast choices, so the experimental process is cut out for you.

- Even if you rent the item across the state, you can certainly have it shipped right to your doorstep. You do not have to drive a long time in search of an item to use.

- Renting is perfect for those people who live in flats or apartments or are without ample storage room. If you only plan to go backpacking once or twice a year, you do not need to have a space for certain bulky items such as the sleeping bags or tents.

- If you go on backpacking abroad, you do not have to carry a lot of items overseas. You may simply head to a rental shop close to the camping site.

The only disadvantage to be considered here is that if you plan to go backpacking often, renting may be a bit pricey. Should this be your case, you can slowly save money for one backpacking item at a time.

Larry Fisher

Chapter 5

The Ultimate Backpacking Apps For You

Apart from the tangible items you need to prepare yourself with before travelling, you will also need to get equipped with the best travel applications out there to keep the experience worry-free and hassle-free. The best apps can be used even when not connected to the Internet. Moreover, you may also quickly download these apps for a fraction of the price or completely free of charge.

1. <u>XE Currency conversion app</u> – When crossing borders or visiting multiple countries, dealing with a number of currencies may be confusing. Moreover, exchange rates may change just in a matter of days. Having a

quick tool you can use will come in handy at any point during the trip. This application is capable of showing more than 30,000 currency charts, the rate high and lows within a given time period, and the rates that are trusted by users. You can also do an instant conversion of any amount between any two currencies to get a quick understanding of how far or short your money will spread in the given country you are travelling. To reset the settings all you need to do is to shake the device. Best of all, you do not have to be connected to the Internet to use the device. This application can be downloaded easily by Android and iOS users.

2. <u>Hostelworld</u> - This is one of the two biggest hostel booking sites in the world. The app is particularly helpful as it can give information in real time. The application lets users book a room or a bed in any of its 35,000 affiliate hostels in different parts of the world. The hostels may range from the most chic to the most affordable. The app also boasts it has more than 3 million reviews and guarantees no hidden

charges. Cancellations can also be made easily. With a mere click of a button, you can immediately cancel your booking without any hassle. For users of Apple watch, you may also receive updates from time to time. This application can be downloaded for fee.

3. Pocket – This application lets users save articles, videos, and even webpages to be read later. This is one of the best 'offline reader' applications and is chosen to be one of the favorites in the App Store. There are now about 12 million Pocket users and many of them are backpackers. Pocket allows users to view their saved articles or videos using their phones or tablets even when not online. This application can also be used with other apps and is equipped with easy-to-navigate features.

4. Tiny Flashlight – You can never tell when you will need a bit of lighting help during a trip. This application makes use of an LED light that can be utilized on different screen modes. It also comes with plugins such as blinking light, police light or a strobe

light to offer the best effects; you can bring the party to the campsite! With this application, there is virtually no need to carry around another flashlight, although it is still recommended to have a separate one on backup to preserve the battery of your phone. This is completely free for iOS users.

5. Skyscanner – One of the most important apps to use when exploring a region through backpacking is Skyscanner. This app helps you navigate through millions of possible flights across the globe. There are now roughly 35 million users of Scanners and these people have all been enjoying countless savings in travel expenses. Finding the cheapest flight for your backpacking journeys is essential so you can stretch your budget further and explore more places. You can look at it this way – the best planned trip and all of your savings for your budget both begin with an affordable and properly booked flight, since this will be your biggest expense by far. The app does not require Internet connection and you can virtually search anywhere for cheap flights.

6. Language – Crossing borders or going abroad can also inevitably lead you to cases of language barriers. Although you may easily find translator apps online, there may only be very few that work well offline. One example is Language, a translating application that you can use for whichever country you may be in. This application offers translated expressions in no time and comes with a quick search function. Moreover, it also has 12 different language dictionaries. Common travel expressions are also included in this application. Best of all, the app can be used with ease on iOS or Android devices.

7. Trail Wallet – Scared of going overboard with your travel expenses? You do not need to worry anymore because the application called Trail Wallet can help you manage your expenses with ease. This application was built by travelers and they know exactly what the challenges are of expeditions on a budget. The developers of this application aim to provide backpackers with a tool that is easy to navigate. You

can first use it by allocating a budget by trip and key in a budget by day. The rest can be taken care of by the application.

8. <u>Skype</u> – You can never go far without making a quick call or two to your loved ones back home to let them know that you are ok, how you are you enjoying your trip, and all the exciting finds you are discovering. The best way to do that is by taking advantage of Internet-based call applications such as Skype. You can also make a quick international call using the same application for only minimal credits. This is also an excellent way to get in touch with your banks, travel agency, and insurance providers when something odd comes up during your trip.

9. <u>Back Tracker -</u> This is one of the applications that is now gaining ground among the communities of backpackers. It is described as an interactive space or journal where you can save photos, journal entries, travel highlights, and eventually share them with friends or loved ones back home. It is also now

considered to be the top backpacking virtual catalog for every type of traveler. Information included in this virtual journal can be quickly linked to Facebook, Instagram, and Twitter. Privacy settings can also be changed quickly.

10. <u>Prey Project</u> – This is an application that offers added security and protection to your devices. This is basically is a tracking device that can help you trace your stolen device when travelling. Apart from its tracing ability, the app also prevents your phone from getting hacked or accessed. When a device gets lost, you may simply track it using another device such as your laptop or tablet.

Larry Fisher

Chapter 6

Becoming A True Backpacking Pro And World-class Traveler

Ok Globetrotter, so you have got down the essentials and the basics of packing. You are wiser to the ways of stretching your dollar when it comes to transportation, finding a place to stay and keeping yourself well-fed. You even have a starter list for beautiful and interesting places to start exploring that you otherwise may have not been aware of or have had reservations about because you did not know enough. Now it is time to take it to the next level and squeeze out the essence of what it takes to become a full-fledged, well-rounded and streetwise backpacker. Are you ready? Let's go.

Preparation on the Next Level

We all live on an amazing, subtly vibrant and revolving planet that most of us would like to get to know better and are willing to invest an extent of our lives into doing so, even if it means venturing into the unknown with little more than a 12 kilo or 25 lbs backpack strapped to our shoulders and the curious spirit of exploration to lead us into such territory. The world is circular, it spins, and as it rotates it still cycles in an even larger rounded formation. Each time it passes around we may feel like we have not moved much ourselves, yet we have gained so much more knowledge, wisdom and experience within that cycle as we return back to the beginning. And so it goes within this book that as you have come so far and picked up so much or even just a bit more knowledge depending on your experience level, we return to the beginning for a new cycle of preparation.

Now that you know several methods for survival and making the most out of your backpacking trip on a tight budget, to *really* get the most out of your experience you will want to open yourself up as much as possible to just what this new way of life you are entering has to offer. This means doing your research into the culture of the place that you will be a part of for the given time that you are there, so that you can bring the enigmatic treasures of that place and what it had to offer you back home as part of a new you.

Cultural History and Background

Go beyond the practical. Learn a bit of history about the culture of the area you are going to before you leave to pick up a sense of how it has become the culture it is today. Find out a few fun facts about the architecture, the daily life of the kinds of people you will be meeting and any common celebrations there that you have not heard of before. Get into a bit of the folklore if you can. Even if it may seem archaic as remnants of stories past in today's world, it has still shaped that way of life into what it is today. It has created subtle nuances in the mindsets of the people there that affect the way they see life, which is very likely a different way than you see it. For example much of United States and European (particularly English, Scottish, Irish and Western European) lifestyle and mentality comes from an agricultural background. This can actually be said about many cultures, but there are subtle differences.

The evidence is found in our common phrases and proverbs: "A bird in the hand is worth two in the bush," (Appreciate what you already have rather than what seems better that is out of reach), "You reap what you sow," (The intention of your actions and words will come back to you in life the same way that you put them out there), "Money does not grow on trees," (You have to work in order to provide for yourself and others; you cannot always expect things to just be handed to you). If you noticed, all of these common phrases refer to nature, hunting and farming to illustrate belief systems that throughout time and repetition create the mentality of a culture. Take the last one, "Money does not grow on trees," for example: Americans in the United States truly take this one to heart where the culture has become founded upon the belief that every individual has the power to create their own success from just a tiny seed or dream and must work at it to turn it into a reality.

If you can learn to see the way that others do from a different background, it provides more than just a feeling, but a development of knowing a greater wisdom and sense of fulfillment; about yourself, about the world around you and the more you travel, about neighboring worlds that you begin to connect with. This in essence is what travelling is all about, and I am sorry to say but nevertheless I am happy to share with you that the more you come to know this subtleness, the more you will get hooked into the travelling lifestyle.

Language

As you have seen from the proverb examples illustrated previously, languages form an intrinsic part of a country's culture. No two languages are the same, even if they technically use similar words and grammar. It is funny, hilarious even about what differences there are between English language use in Great Britain compared to the English used in Canada or the United States, likewise the differences in Spanish spoken in Spain versus that expressed in Mexico versus Costa Rica versus Nicaragua and so on.

It is advised that as part of your preparation in travel, you would do well to learn some of the language of the country that you will be going to. You do not have to expect to learn it fluently, but memorizing a few words and a few phrases here and there before you go will open up your experience abroad to a whole new level, even with just a little effort. You could get a small pocket dictionary, learn from the apps on your smartphone, invest in a Rosetta Stone program if you are more serious about it or borrow one from a friend who already has it. Since you will be getting into the mentality and preparing for your trip months ahead of time, you can spend as little as 10 minutes a day up to two hours a week familiarizing yourself with the language without breaking a sweat. Do you feel like you are the type of person who cannot learn a language? Well you already speak one, don't you? Your brain possess the skills and doing just a little research online for 'learning languages for the linguistically impaired' will provide you with simple, easy methods to build a small vocabulary and phrase bank before you take off.

Learning the language of the country you will be travelling to is the key to opening up the rich mysteries of that culture. Knowing a few phrases can make it fun and expand your experiences to meeting and engaging more people along the way, not to mention showing respect. You will also find that you will feel more comfortable interacting with people when you know a bit of the common words they speak. Wherever you go, it does not matter, the locals will notice that you are making an effort and more often than not, they will be willing to bridge the gap in helping you out whether it is asking for directions, a cool spot to hang out, a nice place to eat, or just trying to make conversation.

You will be showing the people respect for being courageous enough to visit their country and making an effort to acclimate to it. In turn, you will be pleasantly surprised at how warm and friendly the local people will be with you and also how they will make the effort to speak your language. Learning a bit of your destination's language opens doors you may have never thought were there to begin with, so make the effort to truly reap what you sow and get the most out of your time there.

Geographical Area

This one may go without saying, however let's expand a little context into the idea of being familiar with the area you will be travelling to. If you know your country's destination and the cities, towns, forests, jungles, beaches, or mountainous regions you would like to go to, then it would also do you one better to look up the surrounding area of each of these places and see what they have to offer. This will help you develop a broader sense of what is around your primary destination spots so that you can expand your activity options once you are there.

Have you ever noticed that you feel more at home and more comfortable when talking to somebody if you are able to relate to the various little areas and hot spots that you or the other person knows about in your nearby surroundings? It makes sense because it gives you a better sense of orientation so that you do not feel lost or unconscious about your immediate vicinity. It also gives you more to talk about with another person and perhaps allows you to pick up on some new and interesting things to do or provides you with an unfamiliar and somewhat hidden place to check out in relation to those things you are already familiar with. You can use this same principle when traveling abroad by familiarizing yourself with some of the nuanced places and monuments in the area before you leave so that when you get there, you will feel more confident already.

Streetwise Smarts

These are a few simple tips and rules to go by so that you can have an edge in the streets and keep yourself protected from people who may try to take advantage of you at your own expense while on your trip.

- Beware of pickpockets – the amount of pickpocketing incidents will vary from place to place, but as long as you are prepared, you will not become a target. Keep a lookout for suspicious activity.

- Do not leave important or valuable items in the outer pockets of your backpack – this includes your wallet, iPhone or mp3 player, camera and passport. By being in public places with your backpack on you, you will not always be able to keep watch of a sly pickpocket trying to reach into one of the convenient pockets on the outside of your bag for valuables. Keeping things in the inner core of your bag is okay. Keep your camera on a cord or lanyard around your neck underneath your shirt or in a fanny pack at your hip. You can keep your iPhone or mp3 player here too, or just keep them buried beneath the surface in your bag.

- Make it a rule: fill your front pockets only! Back pockets are easy targets for thieves. Keeping your wallet and passport in your front pants or shorts pockets will allow you to be more aware of them at all times, and when on public transportation or in busy town squares, you can always keep your hands in or around your front pockets so that nobody tries anything sneaky.

- Keep your passport with you always – Always, always. Your passport is your golden ticket when travelling abroad. If you lose it or it gets stolen, you are in for a heap of headaches in finding your country's embassy, waiting to figure out the small windows of time that they are open, and going through a slew of waiting and bureaucracy to get a new or temporary one. It immobilizes you, quite literally, because you feel panicked when it happens too. You can keep your passport in your front pants pocket, in a fanny pack that remains somewhat concealed underneath your clothing, or in a specialized belt that has sewn-in pockets that you can keep it in around the front of your waist.

- Know who to hand your passport over to – Border patrol guards and airport security are the **only** two officials that you should actually hand your passport over to. For booking certain things like a hostel room or bicycle to rent you may be asked for your passport number, so in such a case you can read it off to the person. You should know though that unfortunate as it may be, there are corrupt police and public transport controllers that sometimes take advantage of tourists and travelers if they can find reason to. Do not give them that reason.

Buy tickets or extended passes and make sure they are valid when using public transportation. Do not ever hand your passport over to police or transport controllers, even if they ask you for it, because they do not have the right to take it. Do not even show it to them. If they keep pressing you or threatening you, they are most likely just looking for a bribe. Just stick to the story that you left your passport at your hostel. If you have done nothing wrong, they will eventually have to leave you alone and let you go on your way. Prepare yourself by looking further into the laws and regulations as a tourist in the country you are in with your particular visa if you have one. Be wise, and stay safe.

By keeping informed tabs on the area of your destination, you empower yourself to have a safe and hassle-free time. Learning a bit of the language of the country that you are going to will open doors for you in many ways, adding to the luster of the trip that you are cultivating for yourself. Immersing yourself in as much of the culture of your destination of choice in the preparations stages and during your time there is ultimately what traveling is all about. You will see it in the eyes of the people when they recognize that you are there to enjoy yourself and enjoy their way of life, and they will see it in your eyes with the radiance you give off from having such an inspired time.

Larry Fisher

Conclusion

There are several reasons why people should start embracing the idea of backpacking. Apart from the life-enriching experience that you will come across and bring back home with you, travel can also help you comprehend the joys of existing and meeting with other people amidst the rather impersonal ubiquity of e-mails, video games, and Internet as a whole.

The hesitations that a person may feel toward backpacking are natural. This is due to the comfort that one has already built within his or her own environment. In traveling, we do not only leave a familiar place to go and explore an unknown one, we also set aside our habitual conveniences and comforts along with the daily pleasure they provide. This can be just too much to sacrifice to some people.

However, as the discovery starts to take place by one city after another, one country after another and so on, we tend to value the principle of coexistence even more. This is probably the best lesson that every backpacker gets to discover for himself and herself. This is also why backpacking can be extremely addictive for many people. They start with one city, and the next thing you know, they want to conquer the world.

I hope that you enjoyed reading this book as much as I enjoyed writing it. To be able to consolidate all the tips and backpacking hacks for you was more pleasurable than it may seem, that is until you go on your own adventure and get the experience for yourself. Then you can share your life-expanding encounter with your friends and perhaps inspire them to go on a trip of their own, or go along with you on your next one! When you do, be sure to share this book with them too and all that you have learned. I hope that this book was able to help you address those issues on backpacking that matter the most. Moreover, I hope that this book would also help you explore the world in greater heights, in better ways, and at exciting new levels.

Enjoy travelling and enjoying exploring our only planet. Go backpacking and see what this beautiful world has to offer you and me.

Larry Fisher

Made in the USA
San Bernardino, CA
25 April 2016